THE ULTIMATE ANIMAL LIBRARY

Platypuses

by Janie Scheffer

BLASTOFF! READERS 2

BLASTOFF! READERS, AN IMPRINT OF BELLWETHER MEDIA BY FLUTTERBEE

Blastoff! Readers are carefully developed by literacy experts to build reading stamina and move students toward fluency by combining standards-based content with developmentally appropriate text.

LEVELS

Level 1 provides the most support through repetition of high-frequency words, light text, predictable sentence patterns, and strong visual support.

Level 2 offers early readers a bit more challenge through varied sentences, increased text load, and text-supportive special features.

Level 3 advances early-fluent readers toward fluency through increased text load, less reliance on photos, advancing concepts, longer sentences, and more complex special features.

★ **Blastoff! Universe**

Reading Level

Blastoff! Beginners — Grade K

Blastoff! Readers — Grades 1–3

Blastoff! Discovery — Grade 4

This edition first published in 2027 by Bellwether Media, Inc.

For information regarding permission, write to Bellwether Media, Inc., Attention: Permissions Department, 3500 American Blvd W, Suite 150, Bloomington, MN 55431.

Library of Congress Cataloging-in-Publication Data is available at www.loc.gov or upon request from the publisher.

ISBN: 9798898800437 (hardcover)
ISBN: 9798898801670 (ebook)

Editor: Elizabeth Neuenfeldt Designer: Brittany McIntosh

Printed in the United States of America, North Mankato, MN.

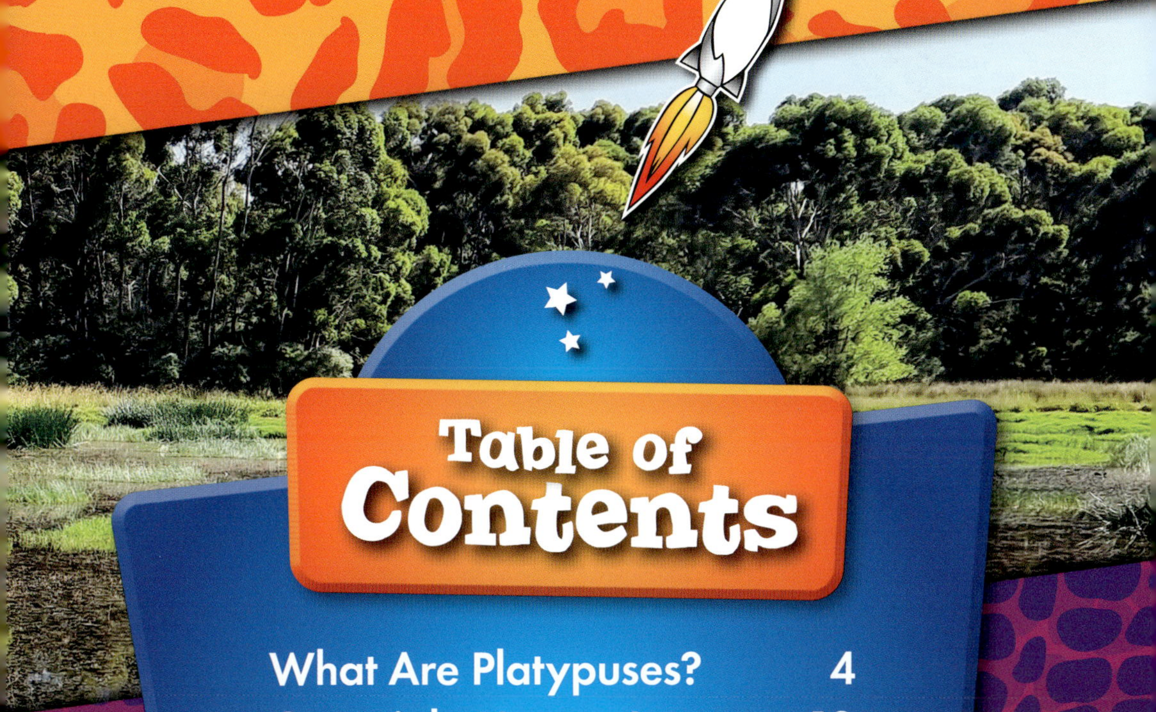

Table of Contents

What Are Platypuses?

Platypuses are **mammals**.
They are known for their **bills**!
They are mostly found in eastern and southern Australia.

Platypus Report

Range

Status in the Wild

near threatened

Habitats

Platypuses are covered in thick, brown, **waterproof** fur. They have white fur under their small eyes.

They have paddle-like tails and **webbed feet**. These help platypuses swim!

Platypuses have claws. They use their claws to dig **burrows**.

Platypus bills are flat and soft. They help platypuses sense food underwater.

Male platypuses have **venomous** stingers on their back feet.

They use these against other males during **mating season**.

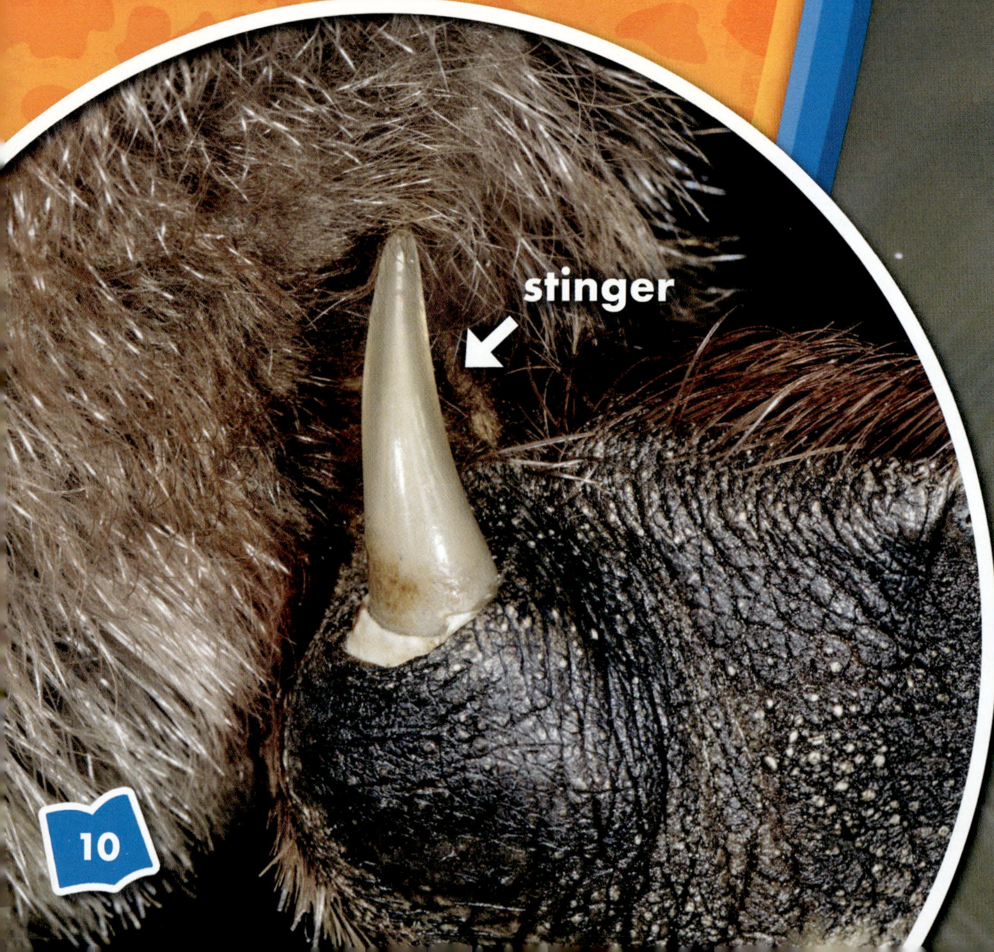

Spot a Platypus

Overnight Hunters!

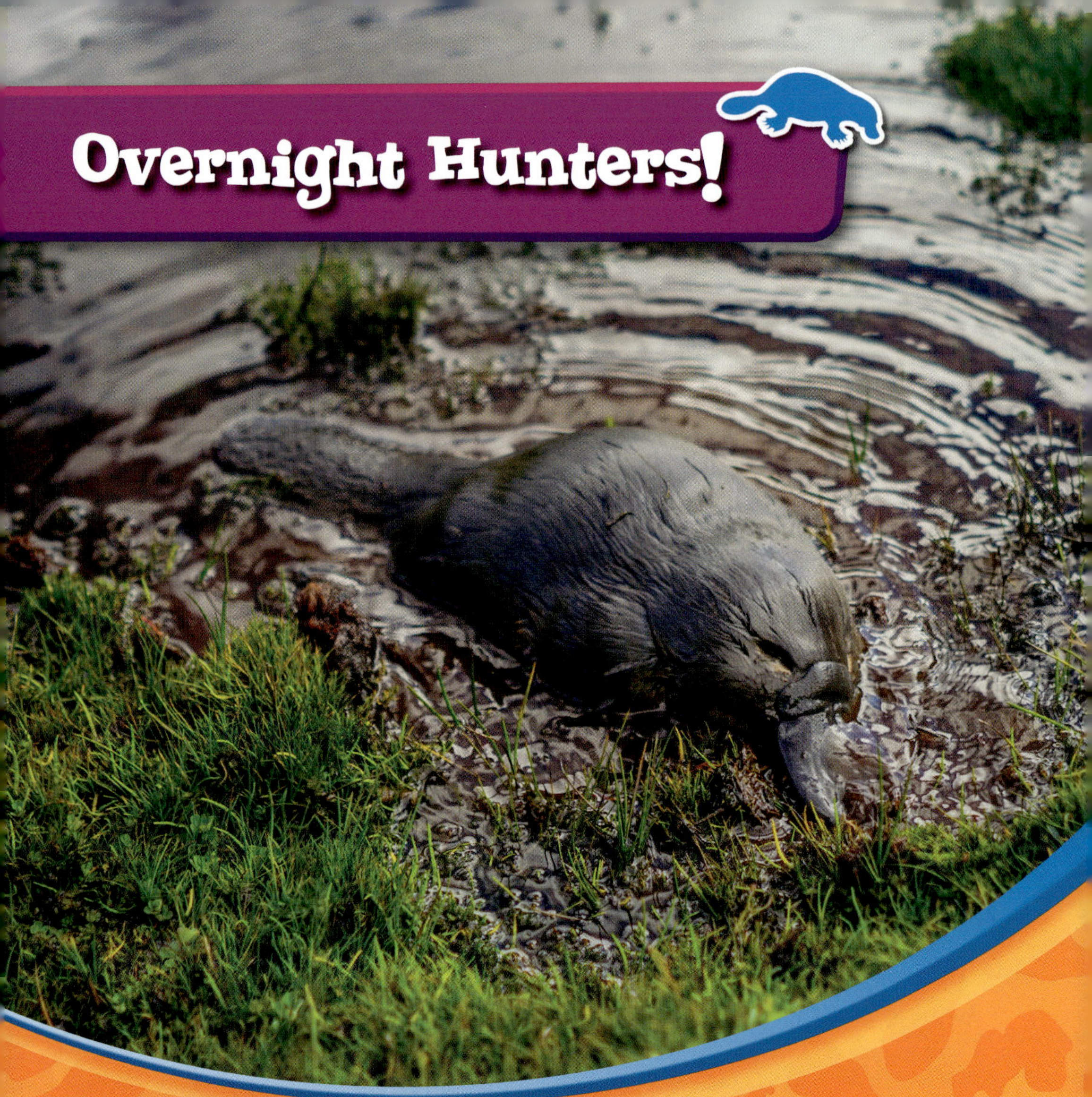

Platypuses live in lakes, rivers, and **wetlands**. Out of the water, they rest in burrows.

They mostly live alone. But they share bodies of water with other platypuses.

Platypuses stay safe from **predators** in their burrows during the day.

They leave their burrows at night.
They swim to find food.

Platypuses hunt for up to
12 hours a night!

These **carnivores** use their bills to find **insects**, shrimp, and worms.

Growing Up

Female platypuses lay one to three eggs at a time. They hold the eggs to keep them warm.

After about 10 days, the eggs break open.

Puggles come out without hair.
They are the size of a bean.

They stay with mom for up to four months. They can live for up to 21 years!

Life of a Platypus

Name of Babies

puggles

Number of Eggs

1 to 3

Time Spent with Mom

up to 4 months

Life Span

up to 21 years

Glossary

bills–the mouths of some animals

burrows–tunnels or holes in the ground used as animals' homes

carnivores–animals that only eat meat

insects–small animals with six legs and bodies divided into three parts

mammals–warm-blooded animals that have backbones and feed their young milk

mating season–the time when animals join together to have babies

predators–animals that hunt other animals for food

puggles–baby platypuses

venomous–poisonous to other animals

waterproof–able to keep water from passing through

webbed feet–feet with thin skin that connects the toes

wetlands–areas of land that are covered with low levels of water for most of the year

To Learn More

AT THE LIBRARY

Gish, Ashley. *Platypuses.* Mankato, Minn.: Creative Education and Creative Paperbacks, 2026.

Mallory, Louis. *Platypuses Sense Electricity!* Buffalo, N.Y.: Gareth Stevens Publishing, 2024.

Olson, Elsie. *Platypuses.* Minneapolis, Minn.: Abdo Publishing, 2025.

ON THE WEB

FACTSURFER

Factsurfer.com gives you a safe, fun way to find more information.

1. Go to www.factsurfer.com.

2. Enter "platypuses" into the search box and click 🔍.

3. Select your book cover to see a list of related content.

Index

The images in this book are reproduced through the courtesy of: woopics, front cover (platypus); Imogen Warren, front cover (background), pp. 2-3; NafiCraft, p. 3; D. Parer & E. Parer-Cook/ Minden Pictures/ SuperStock, pp. 4, 6, 8, 9, 10; crbellette, p. 7; Frank Fichtmueller, pp. 10-11; Logomaker691, p. 11; wernermuellerschell, p. 12; Dave Watts/ Alamy Stock Photo, p. 13; Cezary Wojtkowski, p. 14; Photoshot - NHPA/ NHPA/ SuperStock, p. 15; John Carnemolla, pp. 16-17; Frank Martins, p. 17 (dingo); Susan Flashman, p. 17 (eagle); Martin Pelanek, pp. 17 (platypus), 18-19; P&F Photography/ Alamy Stock Photo, p. 17 (insect); Steven Giles, p. 17 (shrimp); dreakrawi, p. 17 (worm); Ash, p. 18; Jason Edwards/ Alamy Stock Photo, p. 20; Nature Picture Library/ Alamy Stock Photo, p. 21.